祷告 **Dǎo gào (dow gow): pray**

鸟 **Niǎo (NEyow): bird**

耶稣 **Yaysue (YAY soo): Jesus**

竹子 **Zhúzi (JYOO zuh): bamboo**

ISBN: 978-0-9970439-7-6

1 2 3 4 5 6 7 8 9 10 LEO 23 22 21 20 19 18

Printed in China

TALES FROM FuFu's FOREST
The Miracle of Spring

**True Stories
Told by Fictional Characters**

By Eugene Bach & Amy Parker

Illustrated by Hopeful

BACK TO
归耶路撒冷
JERUSALEM

Shan stretched and yawned, then sat straight up in bed. The morning sun had finally fought through the mist on the mountains, and he realized that he had slept much later than usual.

He knew that his parents would be long gone by now. It was the season for picking the rich leaves of spring tea, and the entire mountain community was alive with excitement.

Shan quickly dressed, did his chores, and stepped outside, shaking off the winter chill that still hung in the air. He pulled his coat tightly around him and set off to see his friends in the bamboo forest.

Before he arrived at FuFu's cave, however, Shan found Fay, the Sichuan jay, bowed and weeping.

"Miss Fay! What is it? What's the matter?"

"Poor little fella." Fay shook her head and looked up at Shan. "He's not moving." Fay pulled back her wing to reveal a little ball of fluff.

"Now, what's all the hullabaloo?"

Shan looked up to see Yang the takin and FuFu the always jovial panda hovering over them.

"Oooh, it's a baby." FuFu spoke quietly, maybe for the first time ever.

"His nest should be . . . yep, right here," Yang said, pointing.

"It's not fair." Fay sniffed. "He was just a baby."

"Not so fast there, Miss Fay," Yang corrected. "Now, weren't you just telling us a story about a girl in a well? They thought she was—"

"But she *was* . . . I mean, she *did*." Fay quickly wiped her eyes. "I don't know how it happened, but she was gone, and then—"

"Whoa, whoa, whoa!" FuFu bellowed, waving his paws. "Start at the start!"

"Okay," Fay said, settling in, still warming the baby under her wing. "I was over in Saudi Arabia, not too long ago . . ."

"And I kept seeing this one girl, Ramza," Fay continued. "She was part of a big family. Her dad had three wives, and there were thirteen children in all. They were taught to believe in the Muslim god, Allah, and his prophet, Muhammad. And boy, did they follow every single rule."

"Like what?" Shan asked.

"Well, for one, Ramza wore a burqa—all the girls did—a black garment that covered her entire body, even her face, because they believed that women shouldn't show any skin in public. And when it was time to recite the Koran, or fast for a whole month, or pray the five daily prayers, there was Miss Ramza, right at the front of the line."

"C'mon, get to the good part!" Yang chided.

Fay rolled her eyes at Yang and smiled at Shan. "Anyhoooo, one day at school, a girl did the unthinkable: she shared the story of Jesus with Ramza. It was just a simple Gospel tract, a little story about Jesus.

"Ramza took it and looked at it, but didn't think anything of it. She was a Muslim. And Jesus just doesn't have anything to do with Muslims. At least, that's what she thought."

"That's so sad," Shan said.

Yang grinned. "Just you wait."

"Then one day, Ramza's father surprised her. He told Ramza that she would be getting married—to an elderly man who already had three wives."

"Married?!" FuFu scratched his head.

"Married," Fay answered. "The elderly man had made an offer of marriage, and Ramza's father had accepted for her. Ramza would be the man's youngest wife, even younger than his own *children*."

"Ramza was scared. She certainly didn't want to get married at her age, much less to an old man. But she knew that disagreeing with her father could be even scarier. She begged him, 'Please, Father, just let me continue with school.' He refused. But Ramza couldn't hold it in anymore. She yelled, 'I can't marry him! And I'll run away if you try to make me!'"

Fay paused and swallowed hard. "And that did it," she continued quietly. "In a split second, an uncontrollable anger welled up in Ramza's father. With a single move, he ripped a leg off a chair and swung it at Ramza. He—he hit her. In the head. As hard as he could. Ramza fell to the floor. She stopped moving. She stopped . . . breathing."

A few hushed moments passed before Fay continued.

"Ramza's father called for his second wife, and together they put Ramza into a plastic bag and carried her out to a secret spot in the desert, to a dry well. They dumped that precious little girl into the well, and then they just went back home."

FuFu wiped a tear with the back of his paw. "The very people put on this earth to protect her, turned their backs on her."

"Ah, yes," Yang added, "but the one person Ramza turned her back on would be One who would save her."

"How could anyone save her now?" Shan asked.

Fay shook her head. "I—I don't know. I flew away the second that Ramza's father hit her. The rest, I later heard straight from Ramza's mouth. And I wouldn't have believed it if I hadn't seen Ramza myself."

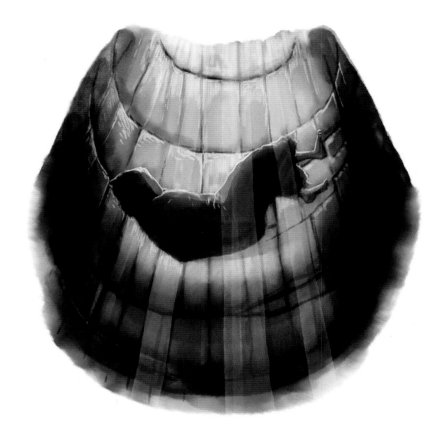

All eyes were on Fay as she went on.

"Ramza said that while she was falling, she could only see a terrible darkness—she believed that she was going to hell. As her life flashed through her mind, she saw her friend at school and the booklet about Jesus. This time Ramza tried to take the booklet from her friend, but she couldn't reach it. Still falling, Ramza then opened her eyes and saw what she described as 'a strong, healthy, and beautiful man' standing at the bottom of the well."

"What she said next, I will never forget." Fay shook her head slowly. "Ramza explained, 'The man caught the sack I was in, then untied the sack, placed His hands on my head and back, and breathed life into me. I opened my eyes as if I were waking from a dream. I saw the nail marks in His hands. I just knew that it was Jesus.'"

"Jesus," Shan said in a hushed voice.

Fay nodded at Shan. "Ramza said that it was Jesus who carried her out of that well. Then He said to her, 'I am the resurrection and the life. He who believes in Me, though he may die, he shall live.'"

"John 11:25," Yang added.

Fay continued, almost whispering now. "Then Ramza said to Him, 'Jesus, I know that You died for me. I believe in You. I am Yours.' But when Ramza lifted her head to look at Him, no one was there."

"So, what did she do?" Shan asked. "She couldn't go back home!"

"Well, God took care of that too," Fay explained. "In a nearby village, a pastor and his wife had a vision, telling them, 'Go to a date plantation where you will find a young woman who needs help.' And that's just what they did. There they found Ramza, praising and thanking Jesus."

"Ha-ha! What about that?!" Yang clapped his hands and kicked back on the rock, almost toppling over.

Shan stifled a giggle as Fay continued.

"And when the couple introduced themselves as Christians, Ramza knew that this was her new family, a family that would be hers for eternity."

"But wait . . . where is she now?" Shan asked.

"Oh, she's still there in Saudi Arabia," Fay explained with a smile, "working with other former Muslims to secretly share about the Jesus who raised her from darkness, from the bottom of that well."

"Oooh!" Fay suddenly jumped back.

Yang readied his walking stick for defense. "What is it, Miss Fay?!"

"He—he moved!" she gasped, and knelt back down for a closer look at the bird she had almost forgotten, right there under her wing.

The little bird tilted his head at Fay and chirped.

She squealed in reply, "It's a miracle!"

"Yes, it is, Miss Fay." Yang grinned. "The miracle of spring."

COLLECT ALL OF THE

TALES FROM
FuFu's FOREST

With more to come . . .
www.BacktoJerusalem.com/store

Every purchase from Back to Jerusalem goes directly to support our missionaries
and projects in the darkest nations on earth between China and Jerusalem.